D1712641

SPORTS
DYNASTIES

NICK
SABAN

AND THE ALABAMA CRIMSON TIDE

BY TOM GLAVE

abdopublishing.com

Published by Abdo Publishing, a division of ABDO, PO Box 398166, Minneapolis, Minnesota 55439.
Copyright © 2019 by Abdo Consulting Group, Inc. International copyrights reserved in all countries.
No part of this book may be reproduced in any form without written permission from the publisher.
SportsZone™ is a trademark and logo of Abdo Publishing.

Printed in the United States of America, North Mankato, Minnesota
032018
092018

THIS BOOK CONTAINS
RECYCLED MATERIALS

Cover Photos: John Bazemore/AP Images, left; Scott Cunningham/Getty Images Sport/Getty
Images, right
Interior Photos: David Goldman/AP Images, 4–5, 6, 9, 22; AP Images, 10–11; Mark Almond/The
Birmingham News/AP Images, 14–15; Dusty Compton/Tuscaloosa News/AP Images, 17; John Mersits/Cal
Sports Media/AP Images, 18; Stephen Lew/Cal Sport Media/AP Images, 20; Kevin French/Icon Sportswire,
24; Todd Kirkland/Icon Sportswire/AP Images, 26–27, 36; John Bazemore/AP Images, 29; John Raoux/
AP Images, 30; Aaron M. Sprecher/AP Images, 33; Julie Jacobson/AP Images, 34; Rich Barnes/AP Images,
38–39; AJ Reynolds/Athens Banner-Herald/AP Images, 41; Vasha Hunt/AL.com/File/AP Images, 42

Editor: Bradley Cole
Series Designer: Craig Hinton

Library of Congress Control Number: 2017962518

Publisher's Cataloging-in-Publication Data

Names: Glave, Tom, author.
Title: Nick Saban and the Alabama Crimson Tide / by Tom Glave.
Description: Minneapolis, Minnesota : Abdo Publishing, 2019. | Series: Sports dynasties | Includes online
    resources and index.
Identifiers: ISBN 9781532114366 (lib.bdg.) | ISBN 9781532154195 (ebook)
Subjects: LCSH: Saban Jr., Nicholas Lou, 1951-.--Juvenile literature. | Football coaches--United States-
    -Biography--Juvenile literature. | Football--Juvenile literature. | Alabama Crimson Tide (Football
    team)--Juvenile literature.
Classification: DDC 796.332092 [B]--dc23

TABLE OF
CONTENTS

1 CRIMSON COMEBACK   4

2 STARTING A SECOND DYNASTY   10

3 CHAMPIONSHIP RUN   14

4 TIDE FOLLOW SABAN'S LEAD   26

5 NFL PIPELINE   38

CHAPTER 1

CRIMSON
COMEBACK

Alabama finished the 2012 regular season ranked No. 2 in the country. Southeastern Conference (SEC) rival Georgia was ranked No. 3. The two tough teams met in the SEC Championship game on December 1, 2012. The winner would get the chance to play in the Bowl Championship Series (BCS) National Championship game.

Alabama coach Nick Saban had already led his team to national titles in 2009 and 2011.

Alabama running back Eddie Lacy celebrates a touchdown with offensive linesman D. J. Fluker.

Eddie Lacy hurdles a defender during the SEC Conference Championship.

Another championship would put this generation of Alabama among the best ever. Georgia wanted a chance to win its first national title since 1980.

Eddie Lacy broke free for a 41-yard touchdown run to tie the game in the second quarter. Ha Ha Clinton-Dix grabbed an interception that led to an Alabama field goal for a 10–7 lead at halftime.

Georgia scored two quick touchdowns to regain the lead in the second half. The second touchdown came when the Bulldogs blocked a field goal and Alec Ogletree returned it 55 yards for a touchdown. Georgia led 21–10 and looked as if it might win the game.

Alabama took the lead again when Yeldon and Lacy scored rushing touchdowns. But Georgia answered with another score to set up the dramatic finish.

The Crimson Tide trailed 28–25 with five minutes left in the game when Alabama running back T. J. Yeldon broke a tackle and made a first down to extend a big drive. Quarterback AJ McCarron had struggled for much of the seesaw battle. But he made the play of the game when his team needed it the most. On the next play, McCarron faked a handoff and threw a deep pass down the left sideline.

Wide receiver Amari Cooper had a step on his defender, and the ball arrived with perfect timing. Cooper caught the pass as he crossed the goal line for a touchdown. The 45-yard strike gave Alabama a 32–28 lead with three minutes left. But the game wasn't over yet.

THE FINAL MINUTE

After each team's offense went three-and-out, Georgia got the ball back with only one minute left and one more chance to win the game. The Bulldogs started at their own 15-yard line but quickly moved down the field. Alabama almost ended the game with an interception, but cornerback Dee Milliner couldn't hang on to the ball. Georgia quarterback Aaron Murray then completed three long passes to get the Bulldogs to the Alabama 8-yard line with only 15 seconds left.

Murray tried to throw another pass. It was tipped at the line of scrimmage by Alabama linebacker C. J. Mosley. Instead of flying to the end zone, the ball fell into the hands of Georgia's Chris Conley at the 5-yard line. The clock continued to run.

Georgia had no timeouts. The Bulldogs couldn't stop the clock. Time ran out, and Alabama won. The Crimson Tide had used great defense and a great running game to

RUNNING WILD

The Crimson Tide set an SEC Championship Game record with 350 rushing yards. Eddie Lacy had 181 yards and two touchdowns. He was named the game's MVP. Freshman T. J. Yeldon added 153 yards and a score.

Alabama head coach Nick Saban celebrates an SEC title with his players.

beat Georgia. They were headed back to the BCS National
Championship game.

The SEC Championship game was just one example of why
the Alabama Crimson Tide was one of the best college football
teams around. Alabama built a dynasty with a tough offense,
great defense, and big wins.

CHAPTER 2

STARTING A SECOND
DYNASTY

The Crimson Tide were football royalty in the 1960s and 1970s. Saban was hired in 2007 to return Alabama to the top of the college football world.

Paul "Bear" Bryant won a national title as a player at Alabama in 1934. He returned to Tuscaloosa to coach the Crimson Tide in 1958 and built Alabama's first dynasty over the next 25 years. Bryant's teams won 13 SEC titles, 11 bowl games, and six national championships.

Alabama coach Paul "Bear" Bryant rides on the shoulders of his team after beating Nebraska in the 1967 Sugar Bowl.

The Crimson Tide went undefeated three times. His last titles in 1978 and 1979 capped a decade of dominance by the Crimson Tide. Alabama won one more championship in 1992 with Gene Stallings. Stallings was the head coach seven seasons, the longest of any coach after Bryant until Saban.

COMING BACK TO COLLEGE

Saban was already a successful college football coach. His teams averaged more than eight wins per year in 10 seasons at Michigan State and Louisiana State University (LSU). He also led LSU to a national title in 2003. In 2005 he decided to make the leap to the National Football League (NFL), but he was unhappy after two years coaching the Miami Dolphins. He jumped at the chance to restore Alabama's legendary football program.

Saban was hired by Alabama in January 2007. His first team finished the regular season with a 6–6 record. It lost its last four games, including an embarrassing home loss to Louisiana–Monroe. The Crimson Tide played Colorado in the Independence Bowl in December. Quarterback Greg McElroy said he saw the team change during those bowl practices. The players were focused on winning the bowl game—which they did, 30–24. That attitude carried into the next year.

Alabama put together a great recruiting class before the 2008 season. A number of future stars joined the program, including running back Mark Ingram, wide receiver Julio Jones, linebacker Mark Barron, defensive tackle Marcell Dareus, offensive lineman Barrett Jones, and linebackers Courtney Upshaw and Dont'a Hightower. That class would go on to produce five first-round picks in the NFL Draft.

In 2008 Alabama started Saban's second season 12–0. The Crimson Tide survived close games with Kentucky, Mississippi, and LSU. They were ranked the best team in the country, but second-ranked Florida upset them in the SEC Championship Game. Still, Saban had Alabama's football program headed in the right direction again.

STAYING UNDEFEATED

The Crimson Tide beat rival LSU in overtime in 2008 to clinch a trip to the SEC Championship Game. Alabama had a chance to win it as time ran out but LSU blocked a field-goal attempt. Rashad Johnson grabbed an interception to end LSU's first drive in overtime. Then Alabama quarterback John Parker Wilson hit Julio Jones for a big play. Wilson scored on a short run to win it.

CHAPTER 3

CHAMPIONSHIP RUN

W ith an experienced defense, Alabama was set for a great 2009. The Crimson Tide easily won their first seven games of the 2009 season. Then the Crimson Tide survived a close game with Tennessee in October.

Mark Ingram's fumble led to a Tennessee touchdown and cut Alabama's lead to 12–10 late in the game. Then an onside kick helped Tennessee get the ball back. The Volunteers

Alabama defensive lineman Terrence Cody blocks a Tennessee field goal in the closing seconds of the game.

were driving to win the game. Tennessee set up for a potential game-winning field goal with four seconds left. But Alabama's Terrence Cody burst through the line and blocked the kick as time expired.

The Crimson Tide kept their perfect record with a comeback four weeks later against rival Auburn. Quarterback Greg McElroy hit Roy Upchurch for a 4-yard touchdown in the final minutes for a 26–21 win.

Alabama went on to play Florida in the SEC Championship Game. The 32–13 win made up for the loss to the Gators a year earlier. It also sent Alabama to the BCS National Championship game against Texas.

Marcell Dareus took an interception back for a touchdown just before halftime for a 24–6 lead. Ingram and Trent Richardson scored rushing touchdowns late after turnovers on the way to a 37–21 win. Alabama was the national champion.

A tornado destroyed parts of Tuscaloosa, Alabama, in April 2011. The Crimson Tide coaches and players helped in the community after the storms. Alabama's run to another national title in 2011 also helped the community heal. It wasn't easy.

Nick Saban speaks at an event to help rebuild Tuscaloosa after a tornado hit part of the town.

The Crimson Tide lost to rival LSU in November. It was an outstanding defensive effort. The No. 1 Tigers won 9–6. The Crimson Tide finished the season ranked No. 2 and got a rematch with LSU in the national championship game in January.

Alabama jumped out to a 15–0 lead on five field goals in the championship game. The Tigers did not cross midfield until the fourth quarter. Dont'a Hightower's sack and fumble recovery ended the drive. Richardson added a 34-yard touchdown run a

Alabama defenders tackle Notre Dame wide receiver DaVaris Daniels during the BCS National Championship in 2013.

few minutes later. Alabama won 21–0. It was the third shutout of the season for Alabama's defense.

The Crimson Tide had an outstanding defense. Alabama led the country in four important categories. It allowed opponents to score only 8.2 points per game, gain 183.6 yards, pass for

111.5 yards, and run for 72.2 yards. The team also won the Disney Spirit Award for its work after the tornado.

TRYING TO REPEAT

The defending national champions started the 2012 season with a big win against No. 8 Michigan. AJ McCarron threw for two touchdowns, and freshman T. J. Yeldon ran for another. Linebacker C. J. Mosley returned an interception for a score in the 41–14 win.

Alabama went on to win its first nine games behind a high-scoring offense and a tough defense. The Crimson Tide needed a comeback to beat rival LSU in November. They trailed 17–14 with 1:34 left in the game. McCarron hit Yeldon for a 28-yard touchdown to win the game. Yeldon took a short pass and got by two tacklers on his way to the end zone. Alabama lost its next game but finished the year with two shutouts. The Crimson Tide then beat Georgia for the 2012 SEC title.

In the BCS National Championship game Eddie Lacy and Yeldon each had rushing touchdowns as Alabama jumped to an early lead against Notre Dame. The Crimson Tide led 35–0 at one point. They won 42–14. Alabama cruised to its third national

title in four years on the backs of one of the best defenses in the country. It allowed only an astounding 10.9 points per game.

Alabama's chance to win three straight national titles ended on the final play of the final game of the 2013 regular season. The top-ranked Tide were knotted up 28–28 with Auburn as the clock ticked down. Rather than accepting overtime, Saban decided to try to win it on a 57-yard field goal attempt. But the kick came up short, and Auburn's Chris Davis was waiting in the end zone. He caught the live ball and returned it 100 yards for a shocking touchdown to give Auburn the win. Alabama played Oklahoma in the Sugar Bowl that year. Alabama had five turnovers and handily lost the game 45–31 to end the 2013 season.

In 2014 Alabama beat LSU in overtime to push its record to 8–1. The next week the fourth-ranked Tide forced three turnovers in a 25–20 win over No. 1 Mississippi State. Alabama throttled Missouri 42–13 in the SEC Championship Game and finished the year ranked No. 1.

The playoff committee chose Alabama as the top seed for the new College Football Playoff (CFP). The Tide were picked to play Ohio State in the CFP semifinal at the Sugar Bowl. Ohio State scored 28 straight points to grab the lead and held on to win 42–35. Ohio State went on to win the national title.

Alabama defensive coordinator Kirby Smart prepares his players before their SEC championship game against Florida.

GREAT DEFENSES

A fierce defense helped the 2015 Crimson Tide win another national title. The team allowed 15.1 points per game and led the nation in rushing defense, allowing just 75.7 yards on the ground per game. Alabama had 49 sacks and forced 27 turnovers. It was one of the best defenses under Saban.

Alabama beat eight ranked teams during the year. Derrick Henry had a 14-yard touchdown run in a comeback win against Tennessee. He broke the SEC single-season rushing record during the SEC Championship Game. He also scored a touchdown when Alabama beat Florida 29–15.

The Crimson Tide finished the year No. 2 in the CFP rankings. Then they hammered Michigan State at the Cotton Bowl in the CFP semifinals. Alabama had four sacks and two interceptions in the 38–0 win.

MOMENTUM CHANGE

Alabama's 2016 senior class set a National Collegiate Athletic Association (NCAA) record with 51 wins over their careers. They averaged more than 12 wins a season and went undefeated in 2009 as freshmen.

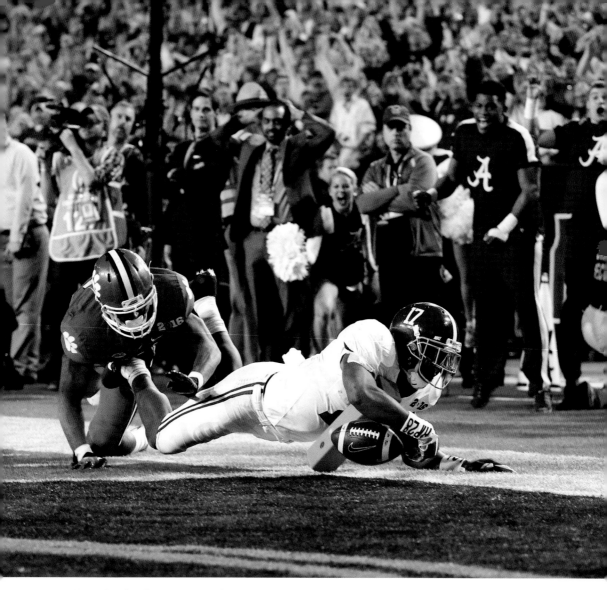

Running back Kenyan Drake scores the winning touchdown against the Clemson Tigers in the 2016 national championship game.

Alabama faced Clemson in the national championship game. Henry had three touchdowns, and O. J. Howard caught five passes for 208 yards and two scores. Kenyan Drake sealed the win with a kickoff return with seven minutes left. He raced down the sideline and dove into the end zone. Alabama won 45–40. The Tide won their fourth national title in seven years.

2016 CHAMPIONSHIP HOPES

The next season Alabama trailed Mississippi by 21 points early. It rallied to win thanks to two defensive touchdowns. The Crimson Tide later beat rival LSU 10–0. Alabama had five sacks in the win. The Crimson Tide finished the regular season undefeated and ranked No. 1.

Alabama won its third straight SEC championship by beating Florida 54–16. The Crimson Tide scored on an interception return and blocked punt to take an early lead. Alabama was the top seed in the CFP. It beat Washington 24–7 in the semifinals. Ryan Anderson returned an interception for a touchdown in the win.

Finally the Crimson Tide faced Clemson again in the national title game. The Tigers scored twice in the fourth quarter to take the lead. Alabama answered with quarterback Jalen Hurts's touchdown run with two minutes left. But Clemson had enough time to score again. The Tigers marched down the field and scored a touchdown with one second left to win the national title.

CHAPTER 4

TIDE FOLLOW
SABAN'S LEAD

There has been one constant during the Alabama dynasty. Head coach Nick Saban has been at the center of bringing the Crimson Tide to the top of the college football world. Saban has proven his skill as a coach and leader. He demands excellence in each part of the program. His coaches and players follow his example. Players and coaches say he is a great motivator, organizer, and planner.

Alabama head coach Nick Saban smiles before playing the Florida State Seminoles.

Saban had a vision for the Alabama program when he was hired. His vision inspired great high school athletes to play for the Crimson Tide. Saban's Alabama teams are known for their physical play and determination. They reflect Saban's coaching style.

Assistant coach Kirby Smart helped build Alabama's reputation as a tough defensive team. Smart oversaw the defense for seven years before leaving after the 2015 season to become the head coach at Georgia. Alabama's defense was one of the best in the country each year under Smart. He won the Broyles Award as the top assistant coach in the country in 2009. Three years later he was named the Assistant Coach of the Year by the American Football Coaches Association.

Linebacker Rolando McClain was already at Alabama when Saban was hired. McClain's play in the middle of the defense in 2008 and 2009 helped start the team's climb to success. McClain led the Crimson Tide in tackles both seasons.

McClain had 105 tackles and four sacks during the 2009 national championship season. He won two national awards for the nation's best linebacker and was named a first-team All-American. Defensive tackle Terrence Cody and safety Mark

Alabama running back Mark Ingram runs the ball against Florida in the 2009 SEC Championship.

Barron were two-time All-Americans on the Alabama defense.

Barron led the SEC with seven interceptions in 2009.

Alabama quarterback Greg McElroy blocks for wide receiver Julio Jones.

That team also had a strong offense led by running back
Mark Ingram, who set a school record with 1,658 rushing
yards. He scored 20 total touchdowns. Ingram's great season
earned him All-America honors, and he became the first

Alabama player to win the Heisman Trophy. The Heisman is given to the most outstanding player in college football each year. Quarterback Greg McElroy threw for 2,508 yards and 17 touchdowns in 2009. He followed that with 2,987 yards and 20 touchdowns the next year.

McElroy's favorite target was receiver Julio Jones. Jones was one of the first big-name recruits to sign with Saban before the 2008 season. He led Alabama in receiving in each of his three seasons on campus. Jones had 58 catches for 924 yards as a freshman. He added 43 catches for 596 yards in 2009, and 78 catches for 1,133 yards and seven touchdowns in 2010.

Linebackers Dont'a Hightower and Courtney Upshaw highlighted another great Alabama defense in 2011. Hightower led the team with 85 tackles that year.

Trent Richardson became the go-to running back in 2011. He broke Ingram's school rushing record with 1,679 yards, and he added 21 rushing touchdowns. Richardson won the Doak Walker Award for his accomplishments on and off the field as the nation's top running back.

A talented offensive line cleared the way for Richardson. Barrett Jones won three national titles at Alabama and played a different position on the line each of those years. Jones was a two-time first-team All-American and earned national awards for his play on the line.

RAKING IN THE RECORDS

Quarterback AJ McCarron was another big part of the Crimson Tide's back-to-back national titles. McCarron threw for 2,634 yards in 2011 and another 2,933 yards the next year. He set a school record with 30 touchdown passes during the 2012 championship season.

McCarron became the first Alabama quarterback to throw for more than 3,000 yards in 2013 and won the Maxwell Award as the nation's best player.

McCarron's running back, Eddie Lacy, and a pair of freshmen energized the Alabama offense on the way to the national title in 2012. Lacy rushed for 1,322 yards and 17 touchdowns during his final season at Alabama. Running back T. J. Yeldon added 1,108 rushing yards for a school record by a freshman.

Receiver Amari Cooper also broke freshmen records with 59 receptions for 1,000 yards and 11 touchdowns in 2012. Cooper would go on to set school records for career receptions, yards,

Alabama quarterback AJ McCarron drops back to pass against Oklahoma.

and touchdown catches. He was named the nation's best receiver in 2014.

The 2012 team had two first-team All-Americans on defense, linebacker C. J. Mosley and defensive back Dee Milliner. Mosley led the team with 107 tackles and four sacks, and he won the Butkus Award as the nation's best linebacker a year later.

Derrick Henry poses after winning the Heisman Trophy in 2015.

MAKING A NEW OFFENSE

Assistant coach Lane Kiffin helped change the Crimson Tide

offense in his three years at Alabama. Kiffin introduced a

faster-tempo offense that featured more passing options. He

had three different quarterbacks in three seasons. Blake Sims threw for a school-record 3,487 yards in 2014. Jake Coker followed that with 3,110 yards in 2015. Jalen Hurts then threw for 2,780 yards and ran for 954 yards and 13 touchdowns as a freshman in 2016.

Running back Derrick Henry was the star of the 2015 offense. He rushed for a school-record 2,219 yards and 28 touchdowns. That total also broke the SEC record for yards in a season. Henry won the Heisman Trophy and several other awards.

Receiver Calvin Ridley recorded 1,045 yards to break Cooper's freshman record. Center Ryan Kelly was recognized for his outstanding year on the offensive line with the Rimington Trophy.

FILLING THE TROPHY CASE

Derrick Henry's historic 2015 season earned him several national awards. Henry became the second Crimson Tide player to win the Heisman Trophy. He also won:

- Maxwell Award for player of the year
- Doak Walker Award for best running back on and off the field
- Walter Camp Player of the Year Award for outstanding player
- SEC Offensive Player of the Year

Crimson Tide defensive lineman Jonathan Allen sacks Florida's quarterback during the SEC Championship Game.

Alabama had a tough defense when it won the 2015 national title, too. Linebacker Reggie Ragland led the team with 102 tackles. Ragland and teammate A'Shawn Robinson were named first-team All-Americans.

Alabama had one of the top defenses in the country again in 2016. Defensive end Jonathan Allen, linebacker Reuben Foster, and defensive backs Minkah Fitzpatrick and Marlon Humphrey were named first-team All-Americans.

Foster led the team with 115 tackles and won the Butkus Award for best linebacker. Fitzpatrick had six interceptions and returned two for touchdowns. Humphrey had two interceptions.

Allen had 69 tackles and 10.5 sacks. He won four national awards for his performance. Allen won two awards for the top defensive player, one for top defensive end, and another for best linebacker or lineman.

The Alabama offensive line also had a top player in 2016. Tackle Cam Robinson was named an All-American and won the Outland Trophy for best interior lineman.

Damien Harris rushed for 1,037 yards, and Bo Scarbrough had 11 rushing touchdowns. Ridley had another big year with 769 receiving yards and seven scores.

CHAPTER 5

NFL
PIPELINE

S aban's Alabama teams have been something of a factory for NFL players since he arrived in Tuscaloosa. Between 2009 and 2017, Saban had 65 Alabama players drafted by NFL teams.

During that stretch, the Crimson Tide had 22 players drafted in the first round. Offensive lineman Andre Smith was the first first-round pick under Saban. He was selected by the Cincinnati Bengals in 2009.

Defensive tackle Marcell Dareus, drafted in 2011, jogs off the field after a game.

Alabama had four first-round picks in three different NFL Drafts. Marcell Dareus, Julio Jones, James Carpenter, and Mark Ingram were selected in the first round of the 2011 Draft. Dareus, Jones, and Ingram were named to the Pro Bowl during their NFL careers. Jones led the NFL in receptions and yards in 2015. Carpenter played in the Super Bowl with Seattle in 2014.

Hightower, who was drafted in the first round in 2012, made two huge plays in two Super Bowls for New England. He stopped Seattle running back Marshawn Lynch at the 1-yard line late in the Super Bowl after the 2014 season. Hightower's sack and forced fumble of Atlanta quarterback Matt Ryan changed the 2017 Super Bowl. His turnover helped the Patriots rally.

WINNING AGAIN

The Alabama Crimson Tide had a great season in 2017 with hopes of another national championship. But just as in 2013, Alabama lost to Auburn in the last game of the year. They missed the SEC Championship Game, and most assumed they missed their chance at another title. However, the CFP committee gave Alabama the fourth seed in the playoffs. They took their chances in the semifinals against No. 1 Clemson and against No. 2 Georgia to win their fifth national title under Nick Saban.

Alabama wide receiver DeVonta Smith celebrates the game-winning touchdown in the 2017 CFP National Championship Game.

Eddie Lacy was also a Pro Bowl pick after his rookie year in 2013. C. J. Mosley and Ha Ha Clinton-Dix were both first-round draft picks in 2014. Amari Cooper was a first-round selection

Nick Saban speaks to the press about an approved three-year extension to his coaching contract in 2017.

in 2015. Marlon Humphrey, Jonathan Allen, O. J. Howard, and Reuben Foster were selected in the first round of the 2017 Draft. They have all been Pro Bowl picks.

Many other players have played in the Super Bowl after leaving Alabama. Terrence Cody and Courtney Upshaw won the Super Bowl with the Baltimore Ravens after the 2012 season. Jesse Williams played with Carpenter when Seattle won the Super Bowl a year later.

SECURING THE FUTURE

Saban signed a contract extension before the 2017 season to remain at Alabama through the 2024 season. He is one of the highest-paid coaches in college sports.

The team's success has helped some assistant coaches get other jobs. Lane Kiffin was hired by Florida Atlantic to be its head coach on December 13, 2016. Defensive coordinator Kirby Smart became the head coach at SEC rival Georgia after the 2015 season. And Jim McElwain was the Alabama offensive coordinator between 2008 and 2011. He left to become the head coach at Colorado State and later took over the program at SEC rival Florida.

Saban's success at Alabama has changed not only the Crimson Tide, but all of college football. Many programs and coaches try to follow his example.

TEAM FILE

ALABAMA CRIMSON TIDE

SPAN OF DYNASTY

- 2007 through 2016

KEY RIVALS

- Louisiana State University
- University of Georgia

SEC CHAMPIONSHIPS GAME RESULTS

- Lost to Florida, 2008
- Beat Florida, 2009
- Beat Georgia, 2012
- Beat Missouri, 2014
- Beat Florida, 2015
- Beat Florida, 2016

BOWL GAME RESULTS

- Beat Texas 37–21 at BCS National Championship, 2009
- Beat LSU 21–0 at BCS National Championship, 2011
- Beat Notre Dame 42–14 at BCS National Championship, 2012
- Beat Clemson 45–40 at CFP National Championship, 2015
- Beat Georgia 26–23 at CFP National Championship, 2017

INDIVIDUAL AWARDS

HEISMAN TROPHY AWARDS

- Mark Ingram, 2009
- Derrick Henry, 2015

OTHER AWARDS

- National award winners: 24
- First-team All-Americans: 37

HEAD COACH: NICK SABAN (2007–)

- Record (through 2017): 132–20
- SEC record (through 2017): 73–15
- National Championships: 2009, 2011, 2012, 2015, 2017

AWARDS FOR NICK SABAN

- 2008 AP Coach of the Year Award
- 2008 Eddie Robinson Coach of the Year Award
- 2008 Home Depot Coach of the Year Award
- 2008 SEC Coach of the Year
- 2008 Walter Camp Coach of the Year Award
- 2009 SEC Coach of the Year
- 2016 SEC Coach of the Year

JANUARY 3, 2007

Nick Saban is hired to coach the Alabama Crimson Tide after two years as the coach of the NFL's Miami Dolphins.

DECEMBER 30, 2007

Saban's first team wins the Independence Bowl to finish 7–6.

DECEMBER 12, 2009

Mark Ingram wins the first Heisman Trophy in school history after rushing for 1,658 yards.

JANUARY 7, 2010

Alabama beats Texas 37–21 in the BCS National Championship.

JANUARY 9, 2012

Alabama beats LSU 21–0 in the BCS National Championship.

JANUARY 7, 2013

Alabama beats Notre Dame 42–14 in the BCS National Championship.

DECEMBER 12, 2015

Derrick Henry wins Alabama's second Heisman Trophy after rushing for 2,219 yards and 28 touchdowns.

JANUARY 11, 2016

Alabama beats Clemson 45–40 in the CFP National Championship.

DECEMBER 3, 2016

Alabama beats Florida to win its third straight SEC championship.

JANUARY 9, 2017

Alabama loses to Clemson 35–31 in the CFP National Championship.

JANUARY 8, 2018

Alabama beats Georgia 26–23 in overtime in the CFP National Championship.

GLOSSARY

ALL-AMERICAN
Designation for players chosen as the best amateurs in the country in a particular sport.

COMEBACK
When a team losing a game rallies to tie the score or take the lead.

DRAFT
A system for selecting players for a team.

DYNASTY
A team that has an extended period of success, usually winning multiple championships in the process.

FRESHMAN
A first-year player.

INTERCEPTION
When a pass is caught by a player of the opposing team.

LINEBACKER
A football position on defense who lines up a short distance from the line of scrimmage.

OVERTIME
An extra period of play when the score is tied after regulation.

RECRUIT
The process of college coaches getting new athletes to join their team.

RIVAL
An opponent with whom a player or team has a fierce and ongoing competition.

ROOKIE
A professional athlete in his or her first year of competition.

TURNOVER
Loss of the ball to the other team.

ONLINE RESOURCES

To learn more about Nick Saban and the Alabama Crimson Tide, visit abdobooklinks.com. These links are routinely monitored and updated to provide the most current information available.

BOOKS

Graves, Will. *The Story of the Sugar Bowl*. Minneapolis, MN: Abdo Publishing, 2016.

Seidel, Jeff. *Alabama Crimson Tide*. Minneapolis, MN: Abdo Publishing, 2013.

Wilner, Barry. *The Story of the College Football National Championship Game*. Minneapolis, MN: Abdo Publishing, 2016.

Allen, Jonathan, 37, 42

Bryant, Paul, 10, 12

Clemson University, 24, 25, 40
Clinton-Dix, Ha Ha, 6, 41
College Football Playoff (CFP), 22, 23, 25
Cooper, Amari, 7, 32, 33, 35, 41

Florida, University of, 13, 16, 23, 25, 43

Georgia, University of, 4, 6–9, 19, 28, 43

Heisman Trophy, 31, 35
Henry, Derrick, 23, 24, 35
Howard, O. J., 24, 42
Humphrey, Marlon, 37, 42
Hurts, Jalen, 25, 35

Ingram, Mark, 13, 14, 16, 30, 31, 40

Jones, Julio, 13, 31, 32, 40

Kiffin, Lane, 34, 43

Lacy, Eddie, 6, 7, 8, 19, 32, 41
Louisiana State University, 12, 13, 17, 19, 21, 23

McCarron, AJ, 7, 19, 32
McElroy, Greg, 12, 16, 31
McElwain, Jim, 43
Miami Dolphins, 12

National Football League (NFL), 12, 13, 38, 40
NFL Draft, 13, 40, 42

Oklahoma, University of, 21

Richardson, Trent, 16, 17, 31
Ridley, Calvin, 35, 37

Smart, Kirby, 28, 43
Southeastern Conference (SEC), 4, 8, 9, 10, 13, 16, 19, 21, 23, 25, 29, 35, 40, 43
Stallings, Gene, 12

Tennessee, University of, 14, 16, 23
Tuscaloosa, Alabama, 10, 16, 38

Upshaw, Courtney, 13, 31, 43

Yeldon, T. J., 7, 8, 19, 32

ABOUT THE AUTHOR

Tom Glave studied journalism at the University of Missouri. He has written about sports for newspapers in New Jersey, Missouri, Arkansas, and Texas. He has also written several books about sports. He looks forward to teaching his children about all different kinds of sports.